Jesus Lives!

The Story of
Jesus for Children

Written by Ron and Lyn Klug

Illustrated by Paul Konsterlie

Augsburg Publishing House, Minneapolis

Dear Parents:

All of us, especially children, love the story of Christmas. It is enjoyable to teach young children of Jesus who came to us as a baby to a manger in Bethlehem. They can identify with the birth of a baby and rejoice that God loved us enough to send us this special gift.

It is more difficult to share with children the story of Jesus' death and resurrection. Death is sad, not joyful, and the idea of the resurrection is difficult to understand.

Jesus Lives! *begins with a story familiar to children — the story of Jesus' birth. Portions of Jesus' life and ministry are included, with emphasis on the love Jesus had for people and how he showed his love and care for them. Events leading up to and including Jesus' crucifixion also are described. The main emphasis, however, is on Jesus' resurrection — Jesus lives! He is alive, and he is with us. He has promised to strengthen us and comfort us, and when we die we will be with him forever.*

The gospel is all *the good news about Jesus.* **Jesus Lives!** *will help your children love Jesus — the baby born at Christmas, the caring and loving teacher, the Savior who died on the cross, and the Christ who rose again at Easter.*

JESUS LIVES!   *Manufactured in the United States of America*

Copyright © 1982   Augsburg Publishing House. Library of Congress Catalog Card No. 82-72848. International Standard Book No. 0-8066-1952-X. All rights reserved. Except for brief quotations in critical articles or reviews, no part of this book may be reproduced in any manner without prior written permission from the publisher. Write to: Permissions, Augsburg Publishing House, 426 S. Fifth St., Box 1209, Minneapolis, MN 55440.

Many years ago Jesus was born in a manger in Bethlehem. Angels sang at his birth. Shepherds knelt to worship him. Wise Men traveled many miles to bring him gifts. He was a very special baby.

Jesus was a boy
in Nazareth.
He helped his mother
in the house.
He helped Joseph in
the carpenter shop.

When he was grown, he began to help people in many ways.
He was a good teacher.
He told people stories that taught them about God.
Men and women, boys and girls, learned to love and trust in God.

Jesus healed people
who were sick.
He made the blind see
and the lame walk.
He even brought the dead
back to life.
Jesus did all these things
because he loved people
and wanted to help them.

Many people loved Jesus too.
They followed him and became his friends.
Children liked to curl up in Jesus' lap
and listen to his stories.

But some men did not like Jesus.
They were jealous because the people
   followed Jesus.
These men wanted to kill Jesus.

Jesus once came to Jerusalem for a holiday.
He and his friends were together in a room for
a special meal.
Before the meal Jesus brought in a pan of water
and a towel.
He washed the feet of his friends.
"From now on," he said, "I want you to help
one another the way I have helped you."

While they were eating the
  special meal,
Jesus took some bread and told his
  friends to eat it, saying,
"This is my body, given for you.
Do this to remember me."
Then he gave them each a drink and said,
"This is my blood
  which will be poured
  out for you.
Whenever you drink
  this, remember me."

After Jesus and his friends sang
          some songs,
they walked to a garden called
          Gethsemane.
There Jesus prayed while his
friends waited in the darkness.

Suddenly out of the dark came
a crowd of men
with sticks and a rope.
They grabbed Jesus and tied him up.
All Jesus' friends ran away.
Jesus was alone with the angry mob.

The men took Jesus back
to the city.
There people hurt Jesus
and decided he
should die.

They made Jesus carry a
heavy cross
to a hill outside the city.
There they nailed Jesus
to the cross,
and there Jesus died.

Jesus' friends were very sad as they took his body and laid it in a grave. A big stone was rolled in front of the tomb. Soldiers stood guard.

Early on Easter morning
some women who were friends
of Jesus went to his grave.
They were lonely because
Jesus was no longer
with them.

But when they came near the tomb,
the big stone had been rolled away,
the soldiers were gone,
and they saw an angel in shining
white clothes.
"Do not be afraid," the angel said.
"Jesus is not here.
He is alive.
Go tell the rest of his friends
that all of you will see him soon."

The women ran back to the city
and found the rest of
Jesus' friends.
"Jesus is alive!" they cried.
Their eyes were bright with joy.

Some of Jesus' friends thought this news was too good to be true. Two of them, Peter and John, decided to see for themselves. They ran as fast as they could to Jesus' grave.

John ran faster, but when
he reached the tomb,
he just stood outside waiting.
When Peter came, he rushed
right in.
Peter could see Jesus'
grave clothes,
but Jesus was not there!

Later that day Mary Magdalene
came to the grave.
She was afraid someone had taken
    Jesus' body away.
As she sat crying, Jesus stood
    near her,
but she did not recognize him.
Softly Jesus called her name, "Mary,"
    and she knew who it was.
She knew that Jesus really was alive.

That night some of Jesus'
    friends were hiding in a room,
    afraid of the people who
    had killed Jesus.
Suddenly Jesus was with them.
"Don't be afraid,"
    he told them.
"I'm alive again.
    I'm here with you."

One night some of Jesus' friends went fishing.
They fished all night but didn't catch any fish.
Just as the sun was rising,
   far off on the shore they saw a man who said,
"Throw your net out on the right side of the boat,
   and you'll catch some fish."

They threw their net out,
and soon it was so full
of fish they could not
pull it in.
"That must be Jesus!"
Peter cried,
and he jumped into the water
and swam to shore.

The fishermen rowed to shore,
pulling their nets full of fish.
There Jesus had a fire ready.
He cooked the fish and served it to
his friends with some bread.

For 40 days Jesus stayed
with his friends,
teaching and helping them.
Then he called them together
and said, "Now it is time for me to
return to God the Father.
Go and teach all people
to live the way I have
showed you.
I will be with you forever."
Then Jesus returned to God.

*J*esus' friends went back
to Jerusalem.
There the Holy Spirit came
to them.
They were filled with love
and went out to help others.
Jesus was with them.

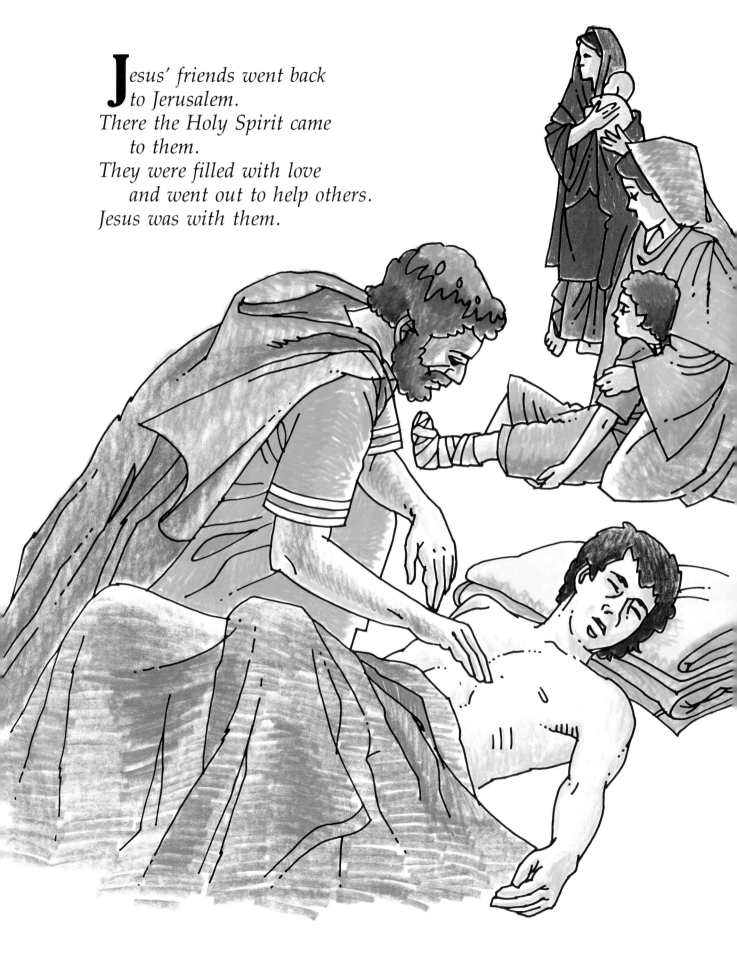

Jesus is with us too,
even though we can't see him.
He is with us when we love
one another.
He is with us when we help
others the way he helps us.

Jesus is with us
when we learn about him,
when we hear his Word,
when we sing praises to him.

Jesus is with us, too,
when we are sick or
afraid or sad.
He heals us.
He makes us strong.
He comforts us.

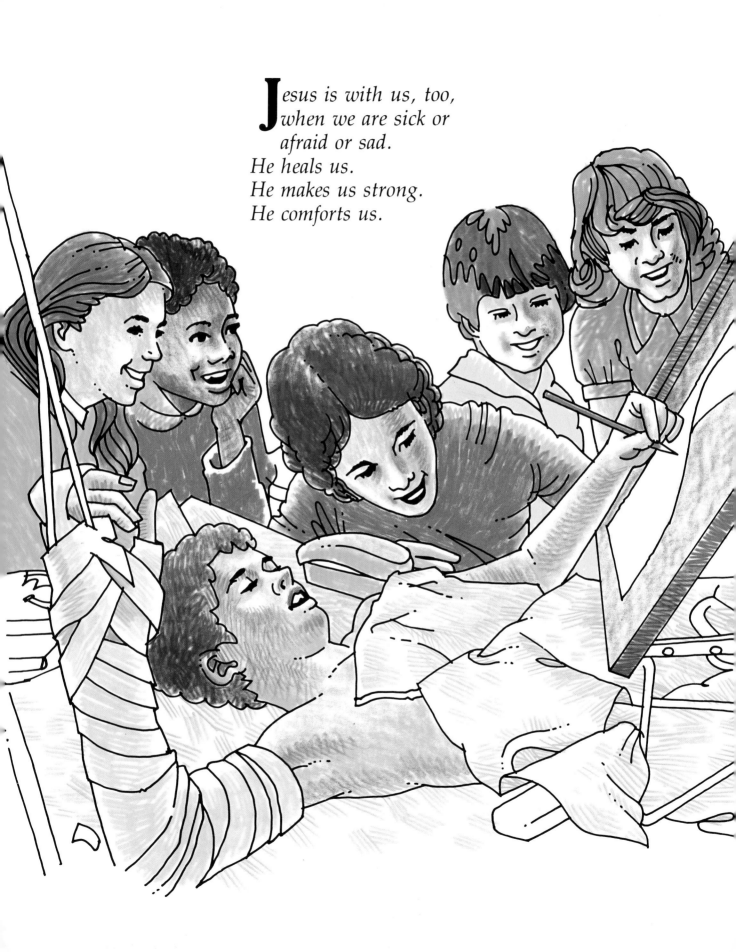

J esus is with us even
when we die.
When our lives on earth
are finished,
we will go to be with Jesus.

Jesus is alive!
He is always with us.
Someday we will be
with him forever.